UP CLOSE

Written by
Isabel Thomas

Illustrated by
Dawn Cooper

wren
&rook

Head to tail

Have you ever wondered what a penguin's tongue looks like UP CLOSE? Or ever been curious about how your hand would size up to an eagle's talons? Well, get ready to find out in this head-to-tail (and occasionally LIFE-SIZE!) tour of our wonderful animal kingdom!

It is thought that eight million different types of animals share our planet. They have some things in common. Many have ears, eyes, noses and tongues to help them sense the world around them. They have teeth to help them eat, and legs, wings or fins to allow them to move around.

There are lots of differences too. Why don't all animal eyes, ears or teeth look the same? Why do some creatures have tiny, blunt teeth, while others have sharp, fearsome fangs?

The answers lie in where and how each animal lives. Over long stretches of time, animals have adapted to better suit hundreds of thousands of different habitats and the challenges they might find there. All those weird and wonderful differences exist because they help each animal meet mates, find food and drink, and avoid getting eaten!

LIFE-SIZE

On the LIFE-SIZE pages, you'll get an UP CLOSE look at two animals who have adapted to live in very different habitats. They have one feature in common – and lots of differences, too. You will be getting up close – so tread carefully and beware of the teeth!

As you read, keep an eye out for mysterious creatures that pop up without explanation. Can you guess why they belong on each page? Turn to the back to find out if you're right!

Look out!

Animals rely on their eyes to find food – and to avoid being eaten themselves! Many animals have eyes with pupils just like yours. Round pupils can focus on objects near or far, while vertical pupils help predators see well in the dark. Rectangular pupils can help an animal see almost all the way around, allowing them to keep a close look-out for predators.

Chameleon

Colossal squid

Owl butterfly

This huge butterfly has fake eyes! The pattern on its wings looks just like owl eyes, which scares off small birds or animals that might want to eat it.

Peacock mantis shrimp

Hammerhead shark

Colossal squid have the largest eyes in the animal kingdom. Each one can grow to the size of a basketball!

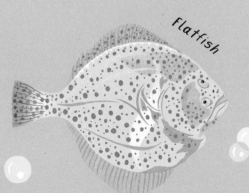

Flatfish

Young flatfish have an eye on each side of their head. One eye gradually shifts to the other side, so that when an adult flatfish lies on the seabed, both eyes look upwards!

Cuttlefish

A fly's eyes are made up of hundreds or thousands of tiny lenses. These "compound" eyes can detect the tiniest movements, which is how they make quick escapes when they sense danger.

Eagle

Ogre-faced spider

Tuatara

Round pupils give animals sharp eyesight. An eagle can see up to five times further than a human!

Peacock treefrog

Have you ever seen an animal with eyes that seem to glow? Foxes have a special layer at the back of their eyes that bounces light back to them, helping them see in the dark.

Goat

Ostrich

Fox

Rectangle-shaped pupils help goats focus on their food on the ground while also keeping an eye out for prowling predators.

A python's vertical pupils widen and narrow very quickly, helping it keep track of its prey while staying as still as a statue.

Green tree python

It's time to put your own eyes to work! Look closely at all the eyes on this page. Can you spot pupils that are round, rectangular and vertical?

Eyes

Have you ever wondered why mammals have two eyes? The eyes are in different places, so each one sees a different view. The mammal's brain puts the two pictures together to create an image of the world that has depth. See for yourself! Close one eye and try to touch the tips of two pencils together, with your arms held out straight in front of you. Without information from both eyes, most people miss the first time!

A rhinoceros has very small eyes for such a big animal. An adult rhino weighs around 40 times more than an adult human, yet our eyeballs are around the same size!

Rhinos are also short-sighted. Over long distances, they can only see about a tenth of the detail that you can! They rely more on smell and hearing instead.

White rhinoceros

Tarsiers have enormous eyes for their size. In fact, their eyes are so large, they can't move around in their sockets, so the tarsier must turn its head to look from side to side. Having forward-facing eyes helps tarsiers hunt. They can work out exactly where their prey is and quickly grab insects, birds and even bats as they fly past!

western tarsier

Listen up!

What can you hear right now? Our ears can collect information about things that are too far away to see, feel, taste or smell. Animals use sounds to communicate with each other, find a mate, search for food, or be warned if danger is lurking. Some animals have ears that do extra jobs, too, such as helping them to balance or keep cool.

All owls have great hearing, but a barn owl's is best. Their flat, disc-shaped faces trap sounds and make them louder. This helps an owl to work out exactly where a sound is coming from when they are hunting in the dark.

Barn owl

Grasshopper

Greater bilby

An insect's ears aren't always on its head. Katydids have eardrums very similar to ours – but on their front legs!

Katydid

Fennec fox

Spiders hear using the tiny hairs on their legs. The hairs are so sensitive that a spider can hear you talking from 5 m away!

Wolf spider

Hippos fold their ears back when they are under water to stop water from flooding in.

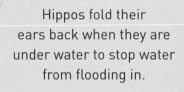

Hippo

San Francisco garter snake

Snakes don't have outer ears, but they can still hear you coming! The bones of their skull pick up sound vibrations and pass them to the ears hidden inside their head.

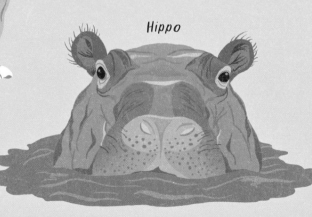

Spix's disk-winged bat

These bats boost their hearing by hiding inside curled leaves. The leaf acts like a trumpet and makes sounds louder, helping them hear other bats up to 30 m further than they can usually hear.

Camel

Water, dust or dirt can damage delicate ears. Camels have very hairy ears to keep sand out.

Caracal

Long-eared jerboa

Each of an African elephant's ears is about the length of an adult human! Their body heat escapes through the thin skin of the ears, keeping the elephant cool.

African elephant

Greater wax moth

Antelope jackrabbit

Sea otter

Fish hear using special body parts, called lateral lines. These pick up vibrations (sounds) that are travelling through the water, and send them to the fish's ears, which are hidden inside its head.

North Sea cod

We humans only use our ears for hearing, but if you could choose, what else would you like them to be able to do?

Ears

Sounds are made when something moves back and forth very quickly and creates vibrations. These vibrations travel through air or water, and eventually to an animal's ears. The quicker the vibrations, the higher the sound.

Spotted bat

Bats can hear high sounds up to 200,000 vibrations per second! To navigate and find food, they make very high-pitched clicking sounds, which bounce off flying insects and back towards them. The bat's huge ears pick up these echoes to work out exactly what and where the insect is. This spotted bat's large ear trumpets help to make quiet sounds much LOUDER.

Birds don't have ears that stick out, they just have openings in the sides of their heads. For most birds, these ear holes are hidden under feathers. But southern cassowaries don't have feathers on their necks, so their ear holes are easy to see.

Southern cassowaries can hear very low sounds, including the deep, rumbling calls made by other cassowaries. If you were walking through the dense, Australian forests where the birds live, you might mistake their calls for thunder!

Southern cassowary

Gharial

Sword-nosed bat

Aardvark

These bats call through their nostrils instead of their mouth. They have a 'nose leaf', which sends the calls in the right direction.

Python

Polar bear

Polar bears have a twisty maze of bony tunnels hidden at the back of their long muzzle. This gives them an amazing sense of smell – they can sniff out a seal 30 km away!

Goblin shark

What's that smell?

Sniff. Snuffle. Snort! Many animals use smells to work out if something is safe to eat. Their noses can also tell them if they have wandered into another animal's territory, or if an animal they meet is part of the family. Some noses and snouts are specially shaped to do other jobs too. Noses have many uses!

Elephantnose fish

Hooded seal

Dalmatian dog

Dogs have very powerful noses! Their sense of smell is between 10,000 and 100,000 times better than a human's.

Silk moth

Mandrill

Albatross

Snub-nosed monkey

Snub-nosed monkeys have nostrils that point upwards, which can be a problem when it rains! They have been seen sitting out in rainstorms with their heads between their knees, and sneezing afterwards to get the rainwater out!

A camel's nose is specially shaped so snot flows straight back into its mouth. No water is wasted!

Camel

Star-nosed mole

The Pyrenean desman is a tiny mammal that uses its long snout as a snorkel while it hunts for insects underwater.

The snout of a star-nosed mole is split into 22 tentacles, which it uses to touch and smell prey in dark, soggy soil.

Pyrenean desman

Whitemargin unicornfish

So many noses to choose from! Which one would you like to try out for a day?

Noses and snouts

Mammals have some of the most sensitive noses in the animal kingdom. A long nose that sticks out is known as a snout ... or trunk! A longer snout doesn't always mean a better sense of smell, but it can be very useful in other ways – especially for animals without hands!

The long, muscly nose of the elephant is not only used for breathing and smelling, but also for all the things we use our arms and hands for, such as grasping, pulling, lifting and hugging. The tip even has parts that stick out like fingers (Asian elephants have one, African elephants have two). This is how a trunk can both tear down branches and pick up tiny things. The trunk can also suck up and hold water, then spray it out again. The biggest elephants would be able to fill a bathtub with just 12 trunkfuls of water!

African elephant

Sengi, or 'elephant shrews', look more like rodents than elephants, except for their long, bendy noses. These sensitive snouts help them find insects to eat. When a sengi is hungry, it pokes its snout into small holes and cracks under leaves and rocks, moving the tip in circles and sniffing for termites and ants.

Elephant shrew

Bills and beaks

All birds have hard bills, also known as beaks. Turtles, tortoises, octopuses and squids have them too. Bills and beaks are shaped to suit the foods their owners eat. But feeding is not their only job – they can also be handy tools.

Australian pelican

Flamingo

A pelican's beak has a huge pouch for scooping up water and fish.

Hornbill

When a hornbill SQUAWKS, the hollow 'horn' on top of its bill makes the sound deeper and LOUDER.

Shoebill

Shoebills fill their beaks with water to pour over their eggs. This keeps them cool in the hot African sun.

Spoonbills swing their spoon-shaped bills from side to side in shallow waters, then SNAP them shut to trap tiny creatures they have disturbed.

Crossbill

Spoonbill

Alligator turtle

Alligator turtles have sharp, hooked beaks for catching prey.

Wall creeper

Pileated woodpecker

A woodpecker uses its beak to hammer on trees, to warn other woodpeckers away!

Eagle

Parrots use their powerful beaks to help them climb.

Stork

Blue and yellow macaw

Hawfinch

This hawfinch's beak can crack open a cherry stone. For its size, it's 320 times more powerful than the bite of *Tyrannosaurus rex*!

Tawny frogmouth

Puffin

Baby blackbirds have a special egg tooth which they use to break out of their egg.

When it's time to breed, a puffin's beak becomes bright and colourful to help catch the eye of other puffins.

Blackbird

If you had a bill that was specially shaped to eat your favourite food, what would it look like?

Bills and beaks

Bills and beaks are tough! They are made of bone, and are covered with a material as hard and stiff as fingernails. But they do get chipped and worn down, so the top layer, just like fingernails, never stops growing.

Compared to their bodies, toco toucans have the BIGGEST bills of any bird. They use their long bill to grab fruit that's growing at the ends of branches. The edges are sharp and jagged like a saw, which helps the toucan peel the fruit. The bill has a second job too. Body heat is lost through its thin outer layer, helping the toucan to stay cool on a hot day.

This tiny bill belongs to a bee hummingbird, the SMALLEST bird in the world. Each type of hummingbird has a bill that is specially shaped to fit into the flowers they feed on. A bee hummingbird's short, straight beak allows it to grab insects and spiders from inside flowers as snacks!

Toco toucan

Bee hummingbird

Open wide!

All teeth are hard, to help break down food, but they come in many shapes and sizes. Meat-eaters have sharp teeth for catching prey and crunching bones. Plant-eaters have flat teeth for slicing and grinding leaves. Animals that eat both meat and plants often have both types of teeth.

Hippo

Snail

Nile crocodile

Slugs have thousands of tiny teeth. As they crawl across plants, these teeth chomp through the plants like a saw. When their teeth become worn out, new ones grow to replace them.

Elephant

Umbrella slug

Wolf eel

Narwhals have just two teeth. A male narwhal's left tooth tends to grow into a long, spiralling tusk, so they are nicknamed the "unicorns of the sea".

Narwhal

Tusks are teeth that grow very, very long! An elephant's tusks are the largest front teeth in the animal kingdom.

Sea urchin

Viperfish

Limpet

It's almost impossible to pull a limpet off a rock, but if you did you'd find row upon row of the strongest teeth in the world! Limpets use their tiny but mighty teeth to scrape food off rocks.

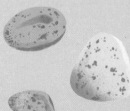

Zebra

Bronze elkhorn stag beetles

Insects don't have teeth, but some have mouthparts called mandibles, used for crushing and chopping food. Stag beetles also use their mandibles to fight.

Walruses

Walruses use their long tusks to fight.

Marmot

A rodent's curved front teeth never stop growing! They gnaw, nibble and grind their teeth all the time to stop them getting too long.

Common warthog

A young tiger's baby teeth get wobbly and fall out, just like yours! Their adult teeth grow a LOT bigger though – the canines can be more than 7 cm long!

Siberian tiger

Goliath bird-eating spider

Crabeater seal

Can you spot an animal that eats meat and one that eats plants?

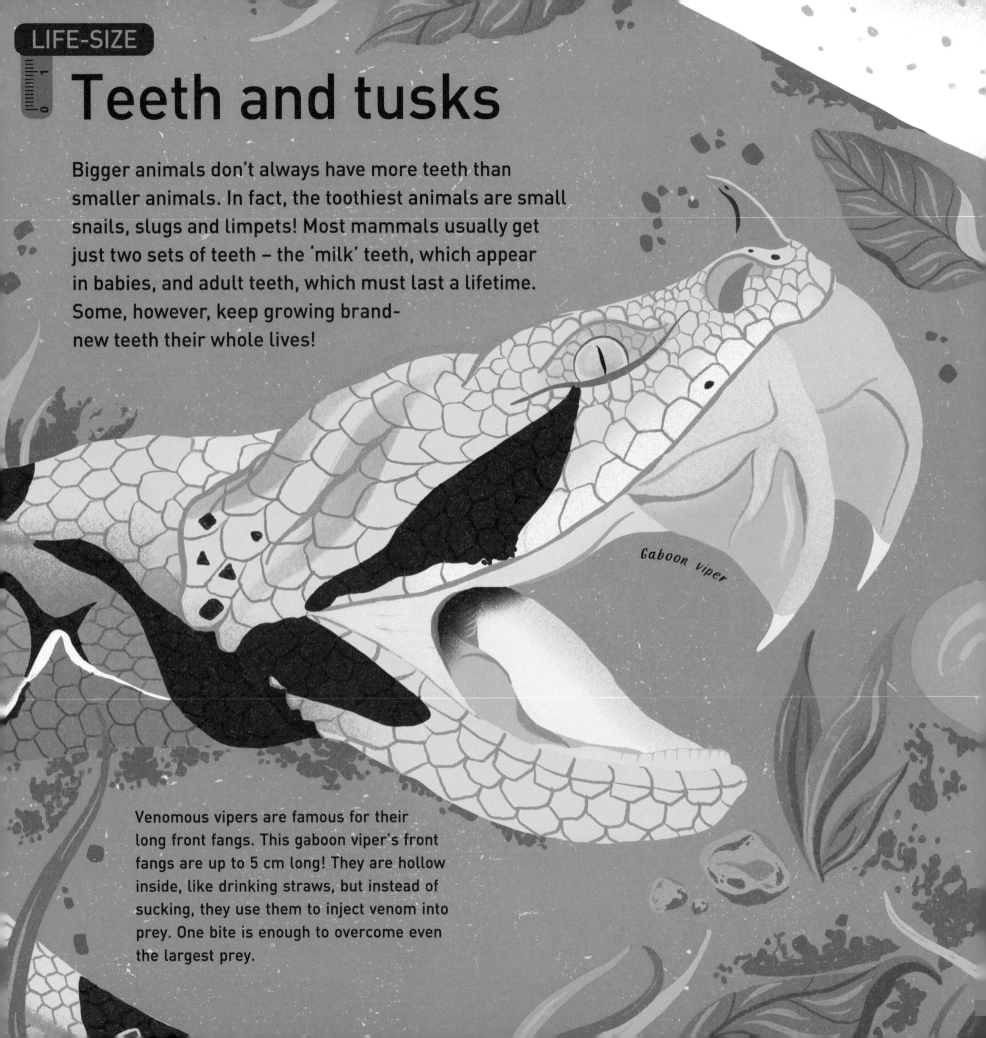

Teeth and tusks

Bigger animals don't always have more teeth than smaller animals. In fact, the toothiest animals are small snails, slugs and limpets! Most mammals usually get just two sets of teeth – the 'milk' teeth, which appear in babies, and adult teeth, which must last a lifetime. Some, however, keep growing brand-new teeth their whole lives!

Gaboon viper

Venomous vipers are famous for their long front fangs. This gaboon viper's front fangs are up to 5 cm long! They are hollow inside, like drinking straws, but instead of sucking, they use them to inject venom into prey. One bite is enough to overcome even the largest prey.

Tiger shark

Tiger sharks can eat almost anything, cracking through shells and slicing through blubber. They have even been found with chewed-up parts of cars in their stomachs! Sharks often lose teeth as their prey struggles to get away. Rows of new teeth are always growing, ready to move forwards and replace the teeth that are broken or blunted. A tiger shark can get through 30,000 teeth in its lifetime!

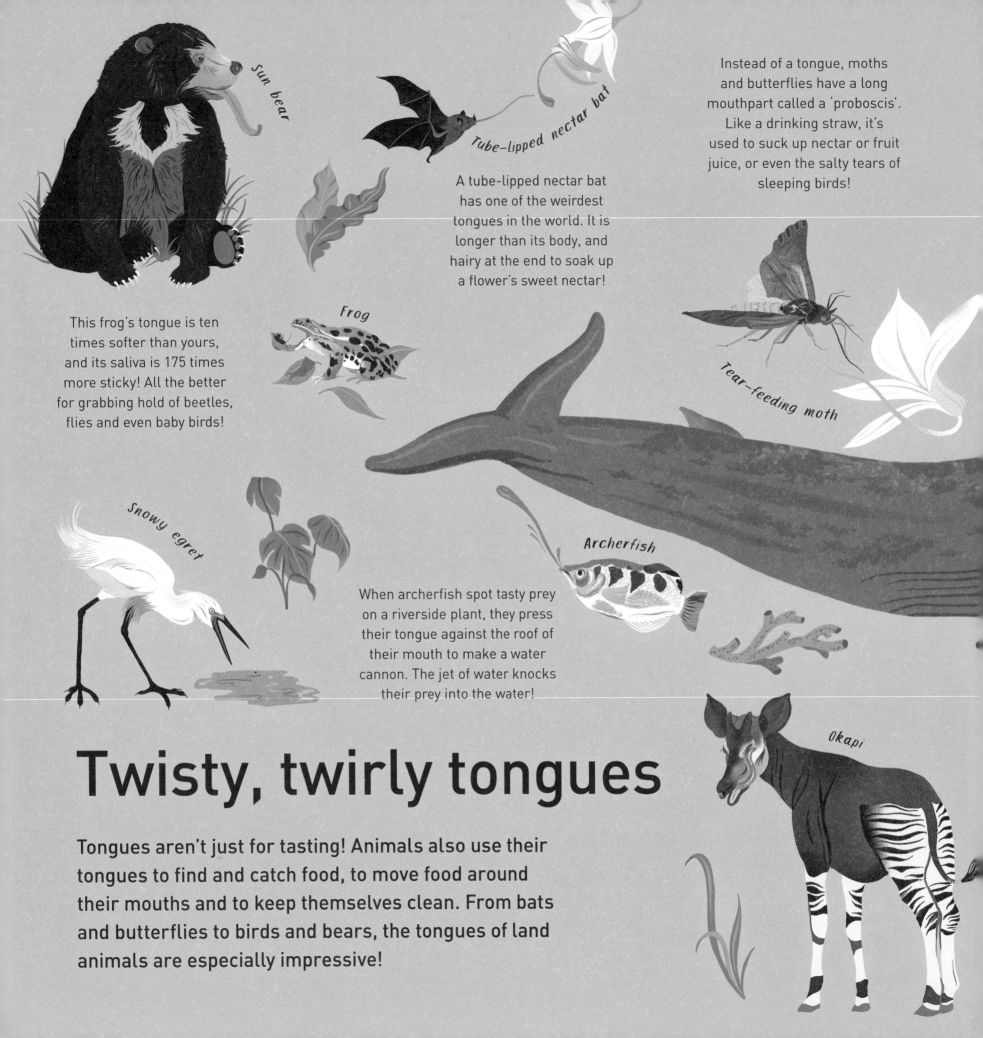

Sun bear

Tube-lipped nectar bat

Instead of a tongue, moths and butterflies have a long mouthpart called a 'proboscis'. Like a drinking straw, it's used to suck up nectar or fruit juice, or even the salty tears of sleeping birds!

A tube-lipped nectar bat has one of the weirdest tongues in the world. It is longer than its body, and hairy at the end to soak up a flower's sweet nectar!

This frog's tongue is ten times softer than yours, and its saliva is 175 times more sticky! All the better for grabbing hold of beetles, flies and even baby birds!

Frog

Tear-feeding moth

Snowy egret

Archerfish

When archerfish spot tasty prey on a riverside plant, they press their tongue against the roof of their mouth to make a water cannon. The jet of water knocks their prey into the water!

Okapi

Twisty, twirly tongues

Tongues aren't just for tasting! Animals also use their tongues to find and catch food, to move food around their mouths and to keep themselves clean. From bats and butterflies to birds and bears, the tongues of land animals are especially impressive!

Lions use their rough tongues to clean themselves and keep cool. Long spines on their tongue help to move saliva deep into the fur on their legs and body.

Madagascan hawk moth

Giraffe

A giraffe's tongue is super-long, perfect for grasping leaves high up in trees. It has a thick and rough surface, which protects it from thorns on the plants the giraffe likes to eat.

Blue whale

The world's biggest tongue belongs to the blue whale – it weighs more than a medium-sized car!

Red-bellied woodpecker

Blue-tongued skink

An anteater darts its 60-cm-long tongue in and out of termite mounds up to 150 times a minute. When it pulls its tongue out, it's covered in tasty insects. It's just like dipping a lolly into a tub of sprinkles!

Komodo dragon

Rosette-nosed pygmy chameleon

Giant anteater

Tongues aren't always pink. How many differently coloured tongues can you spot?

Tongues

For animals without arms or hands, a tongue can be helpful for grabbing food and making sure their next meal doesn't make a quick getaway! Different tongues do this in different ways. Some are grippy, while others are sticky. The difference is due to the spines or bumps on their tongues, called papillae. Stick your tongue out at yourself in the mirror – it has papillae, too!

giant palm salamander

Amphibians have very soft and stretchy tongues. Although they look completely smooth, they are covered in very short papillae less than 1 mm long. Their job is to keep saliva on the tongue, making sure it's always wet and sticky.

The giant palm salamander's tongue is the world's most powerful muscle. It acts like a catapult, travelling out of the salamander's mouth 50 times faster than you can blink. Even a speedy insect has no time to escape!

Penguins have short, tough tongues covered in bristles that can grow as long as your fingernails! The bristles curve towards the back of the penguin's mouth so slippery fish slide in easily but don't slide out again. Penguins have few taste buds, and can only taste salty and sour flavours.

Macaroni penguin

Super-skin

Skin sits around an animal's body and protects the organs inside from sunlight, germs and other dangerous things. Skin also helps animals control their temperature and the amount of water in their bodies. Skin has some even more amazing superpowers too!

White rhino

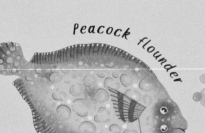

Platypus

Cuttlefish can change the colour and pattern of their skin in an instant! They match their surroundings in order to hide from predators.

Cuttlefish

Electric eel

Peacock flounder

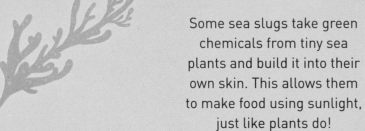

Sea slug

The male mandrill might be one of the most colourful mammals on the planet with its blue and red face – and a brightly coloured bottom!

Male mandrill

Some sea slugs take green chemicals from tiny sea plants and build it into their own skin. This allows them to make food using sunlight, just like plants do!

Golden poison arrow frog

Panther chameleon

Japanese tree frog

Draco lizard

Flying squirrel

With its extra flaps of skin, a flying squirrel can turn its arms and legs into a parachute, so it can glide long distances between trees.

An African spiny mouse's skin tears easily. When caught by a predator, the mouse can wriggle free, leaving the predator with only a patch of their skin! The damaged skin grows back perfectly.

African spiny mouse

Nearly a fifth of a hippo's weight is its skin, which can be up to 5 cm thick! A hippo 'sweats' a sticky red substance from its skin, which kills germs and also acts as sunscreen.

Hippo

Frilled lizard

Corn snake

A Japanese tree frog's skin changes colour at different times of the year. Can you find both colours hiding on this page?

Skin

Skin must be tough enough to protect an animal, keeping useful things IN and any harmful things OUT. But it must also be thin and bendy enough for the animal to move around. Each animal has skin adapted to suit its habitat and lifestyle.

The sperm whale is so enormous, you can only see some of its skin and one eye here! It has blubbery, super-tough skin that helps to protect it from the sharp-toothed suckers that line the tentacles of the giant squid (a sperm whale's favourite food). The sperm whale's skin is more than 30 cm thick in places! From time to time, dozens of whales gather in groups to rub each other's skin. This helps them shed dead skin and get rid of some of the tiny animals that like to live on it.

Sperm whale

Glass frog

Glass frogs live in cloud forests, where their best chance of survival is blending in with leaves. Their skin is the secret to their success – it's slightly see-through on their legs and belly. This makes the outline of their body blur into the leaf, making them hard for predators to spot. You can see a glass frog's beating heart, stomach, blood vessels and bones through its skin! All frogs have this thin skin, which they can also breathe and drink through.

Built-in armour

These animals are covered in hundreds or thousands of scales. They make an animal's skin tougher, and harder to break or bite through. Scales allow reptiles to survive in hot, dry places, because they stop water escaping through the skin. Some scales even help their owner to move around.

Iguanas have at least five different types of scales. The scales along their neck and back are long and stick up, helping them hide among spiky plants.

Blue iguana

Blue morpho butterfly

A butterfly's wings are covered in tiny scales. These are arranged in a pattern that reflects light in lots of different directions, making the butterfly gleam brightly like a jewel.

Armadillos are the only mammals with scales. Their tough scales are linked by bendy skin, so the armadillo can still move around easily.

Armadillo

Arapaima

Burmese star tortoise

A tortoise's bony shell is covered with large, hard scales called scutes. They are impossible for most predators to bite through.

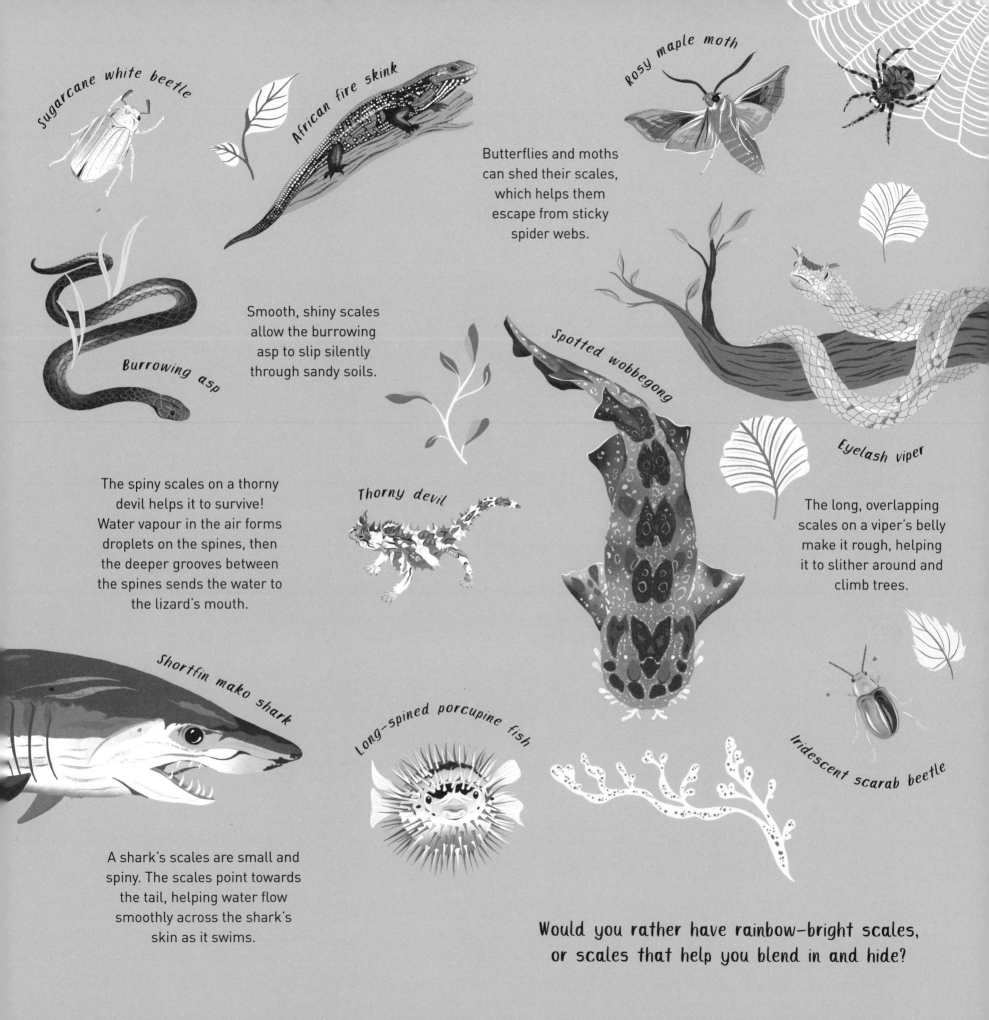

Sugarcane white beetle

African fire skink

Rosy maple moth

Butterflies and moths can shed their scales, which helps them escape from sticky spider webs.

Smooth, shiny scales allow the burrowing asp to slip silently through sandy soils.

Burrowing asp

Spotted wobbegong

Eyelash viper

The spiny scales on a thorny devil helps it to survive! Water vapour in the air forms droplets on the spines, then the deeper grooves between the spines sends the water to the lizard's mouth.

Thorny devil

The long, overlapping scales on a viper's belly make it rough, helping it to slither around and climb trees.

Shortfin mako shark

Long-spined porcupine fish

Iridescent scarab beetle

A shark's scales are small and spiny. The scales point towards the tail, helping water flow smoothly across the shark's skin as it swims.

Would you rather have rainbow-bright scales, or scales that help you blend in and hide?

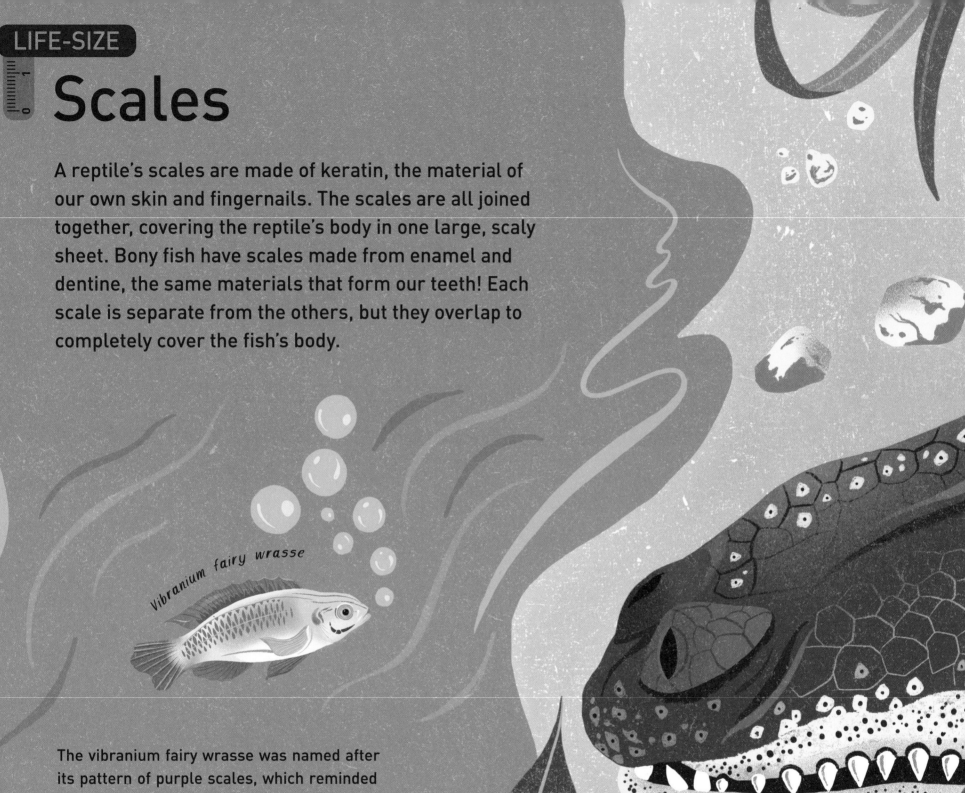

Scales

A reptile's scales are made of keratin, the material of our own skin and fingernails. The scales are all joined together, covering the reptile's body in one large, scaly sheet. Bony fish have scales made from enamel and dentine, the same materials that form our teeth! Each scale is separate from the others, but they overlap to completely cover the fish's body.

Vibranium fairy wrasse

The vibranium fairy wrasse was named after its pattern of purple scales, which reminded scientists of the fictional metal from a Marvel comic book. There are more than 500 different species of wrasse, and many have bright, rainbow-coloured scales. Some even have scales that change colour with their mood. The different colours and patterns help wrasse of the same species to recognise each other.

American alligator

An alligator's scales are different shapes and sizes depending on which part of the body they are found. It has scutes – bony external plates like those on a tortoise – on its back for extra protection. Armoured dinosaurs had these too!

Winged nightjar

Orangutan

Leopard

Alpaca

The flowing fur of an orangutan appears bright-orange in the sun, but in the shade of the trees, it looks much darker.

Cinereous mourner chick

The fluffy feathers of these chicks are a clever disguise. They make them look exactly like toxic caterpillars, which scares predators away.

Kiwi

Feathers and fur

All birds have feathers – and they are the only animals that do! All mammals have fur or hair. Whether feather, fur or hair, these coverings are very important for keeping animals warm ... and they can help in other ways too.

Have you ever seen a bird with a beard? Kiwis have bristly feathers around their beaks that work like whiskers, helping the bird to sense things around it.

Porcupine

Reeve's pheasant

A porcupine's quills are actually enormous, stiff hairs. When it shakes its body, the quills make a noise that can scare away predators!

Rainbow lorikeet

Echidna

Ribbon-tailed astrapia

This ribbon-tailed astrapia's tail feathers are three times longer than its body!

Zebra

A reindeer's antlers are covered with hairy skin known as velvet. This supplies the antlers with lots of nutrients, so they can grow quickly.

Emu

Caribou reindeer

Peafowl

Which animal's long, bright feathers are perfect for showing off?

Fur

Mammals that live in colder parts of the world are often more furry than those living in hot places. Fur traps a layer of air close to an animal's body, stopping heat from escaping. It may also bounce heat back towards the animal's skin. Smooth-skinned marine mammals, such as whales and dolphins, live in cold water. They have a thick layer of fat called blubber underneath their skin to keep them warm. But even dolphins have a few whiskers when they are born!

sea otter

Ostrich egg

Ostriches lay the biggest eggs in the world. However, they are actually the world's smallest eggs compared to the large size of the bird! Each egg weighs around the same as 24 chicken eggs, but this is only one-fiftieth of a grown ostrich's weight.

From top to ... tail!

For animals lucky enough to have one, a tail is a very handy tool. Most tails are part of an animal's backbone, and they can be feathered or furry, scaly or smooth. Tails have lots of different uses, too. They might help an animal to move or to find food. Tails can be used as a weapon, and can also help animals show if they are feeling friendly or fierce!

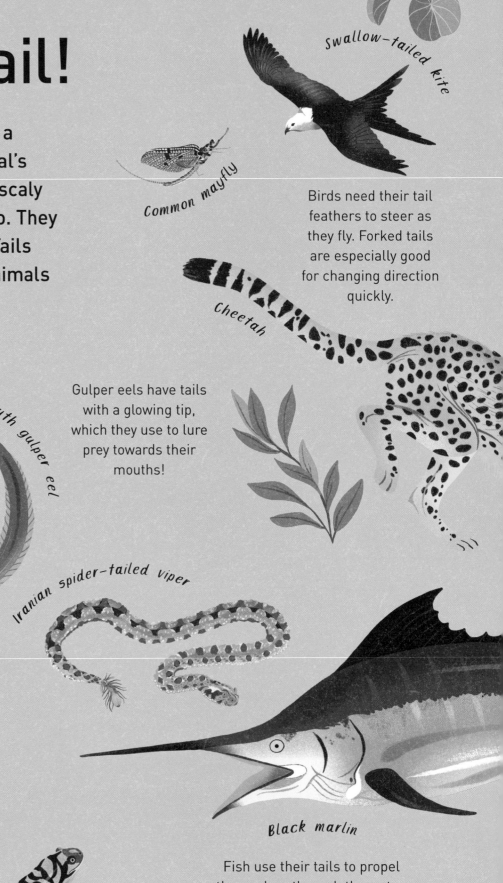

Swallow-tailed kite

Common mayfly

Birds need their tail feathers to steer as they fly. Forked tails are especially good for changing direction quickly.

Cheetah

Umbrella-mouth gulper eel

Gulper eels have tails with a glowing tip, which they use to lure prey towards their mouths!

Iranian spider-tailed viper

Leaf-tailed gecko

The end of this viper's tail looks just like a spider. The snake sits still, and gently drags its tail across the ground, waiting for a bird to try and catch it. The bird then becomes the prey itself!

Black marlin

Salamander

Fish use their tails to propel themselves through the water. Black marlins can travel as fast as a speedy car thanks to their hefty tails.

Greater glider squirrel

Woolly spider monkey

Madagascan collared iguana

Red wolf

A giraffe's tail is taller than a fully grown human, making it the longest of any land mammal.

Giraffe

Bush kangaroo

Pallas's glass snake

Scorpion

Lots of creepy crawlies use their tails for stinging or spraying toxic chemicals. Scorpions use their stings for self-defence, as well as for injuring prey.

Common mouse opossum

If you had a tail, what would you use it for? Just think how useful it could be!

Tails

The size and shape of an animal's tail gives us clues about how they might use it. Although these two animals and their tails look completely different, they both use their tails for the same thing – to trick other animals!

Asian grass lizard

Lizards have multitasking tails. Some can grasp branches as they climb. Others are chunky – they store so much fat that the lizard can go for months without eating. Strangest of all, some lizards' tails break off when grabbed by a predator, allowing the rest of the lizard to make a quick getaway. This Asian grass lizard's tail can do all these things and more. It grows up to five times as long as the lizard's body, which might trick predators into thinking the lizard is a snake!

Naked mole-rat

Naked mole-rats are one of the least hairy land mammals. They find it hard to stay warm, so they huddle together in underground burrows at night. But naked mole-rats aren't completely hairless. Whiskers on their face and tail help them sense what's around them in the dark.

Sea otters are the world's furriest animals. Every square centimetre (which is about the size of an adult human's fingernail) of their skin has around 140,000 hairs. There are two main types of fur, and sea otters have both. The short, thick 'ground hairs' trap air to keep the otter warm in icy water. The longer, tougher 'guard hairs' lie over the top of their fluffy overcoat, helping to keep it dry.

Wonderful wings

Most animals with wings use them to lift themselves off the ground and move through the air. Flying animals need light bodies and large muscles to power their wings. Birds, insects and bats are the only creatures in the animal kingdom that can fly. Not all birds can use their wings to fly.

Swift

Hummingbird hawk moth

Beetles have two pairs of wings, but they only use one pair to fly. The other pair form a hard case on top, which protect the wings when the beetle isn't flying.

Hercules beetle

Birds that can't fly use their wings in other ways. An ostrich's wings help it balance and change direction as it runs.

Ostrich

Horned sungem (hummingbird)

Gull

Rapidly beating wings allow hummingbirds to fly upwards, downwards, sideways and backwards – and even hover in front of flowers to drink nectar.

Dragonfly

True fly

True flies are insects with one pair of wings. They can fly backwards, sideways and even upside down!

Fruit bat

Bats are the only mammals with wings. Fruit bats use their long, narrow wings to fly far from their roost to look for fruit trees.

Peregrine falcon

Albatross

Each of an albatross's wings is about the length of a typical 10-year-old child! They can have a wingspan of up to 3.5 m, which is the widest wingspan in the world.

Sparrow

Ruppell's griffon vulture

A male bird of paradise impresses a female by holding his wings up and dancing around in circles.

Blue jay

Superb bird-of-paradise

Bumblebee

Gentoo penguin

Can you spot a bird whose wings are adapted for swimming, not flying?

Wings

Flapping wings get a bird moving forwards – like an aeroplane on a runway. Once air is flowing over and under the wings fast enough, the bird is lifted into the air. This is why birds can glide for some distance without flapping once they are in the air. Bat and insect wings work a bit differently – their smaller wings take much more energy to flap and fly!

Atlas moth

Atlas moths have the largest wings of any insect. A moth this size would find it hard to hide from birds and other predators, so it doesn't try. Instead, the patterns on its wings mimic the head of a poisonous cobra snake to scare other animals away! Flying with wings this big uses a lot of energy, but strangely, adult Atlas moths never eat! They just use up food stored in their bodies from when they were caterpillars.

Kitti's hog-nosed bat

Bats have very bendy wings that twist, stretch and change shape as they flap. These movements push the bat forwards and lift it upwards at the same time. It's as if they are swimming or rowing through the air. Being able to change their wing shape easily also helps bats change direction very quickly and perform acrobatics in the air! Kitti's hog-nosed bats are the world's smallest bats – they are so tiny they are also known as "bumblebee bats".

Paws and claws

Claws are the hard, pointed parts at the tips of an animal's fingers or toes. Feet with claws are known as paws. We also use the word "claw" to describe parts of an animal that grab and pinch, like the claws of a crab or a lobster. Be careful! Don't get too close, or you might get nipped!

Linnaeus's two-toed sloth

Wallace's flying frog

Kangaroo

Tokay

A kangaroo's back paws are large and long, for bounding quickly. Older kangaroos use their front paws for boxing matches to find out who should be in charge!

Gibbon

Polar bear

Gibbons have short, flat fingernails. These protect their fingers as they grasp things, but don't get in the way when they are climbing and swinging through the trees.

A polar bear's paws are as large as dinner plates. Their webbed toes help them swim, and their curved claws help them grip slippery ice – or seals!

Lion

Plumed basilisk

Long toes tipped with razor-sharp claws help the plumed basilisk run quickly and climb trees. Basilisks are able to gather enough speed to run several metres across water without sinking!

Mountain goat

Jacana

Giant armadillo

Water bear

Female African clawed frog

The largest lobsters have claws strong enough to break a person's arm!

Male fiddler crabs have one gigantic claw. They use it for fighting other crabs, or to impress females by waving it in patterns.

Fiddler crab

Gorilla

Lobster

What differences can you see between your fingernails and the claws of other animals?

Claws

The super-sharp claws of a bird of prey are known as talons. They are useful for catching slippery, wriggly prey such as snakes or fish! Not all animal claws are long, narrow and sharp. Primates such as lemurs have wide, flat nails instead.

Aye-aye

The four black talons on each foot of a harpy eagle can grow longer than an adult human's fingers. A harpy eagle hunts by sitting silently in a tree, watching and waiting. When it spots a monkey, sloth, porcupine, snake or deer, it dives down to hit its target feet first! As the bird grabs the prey, all the force of the grip is focused right at the tips of the talons. The pressure is enough to crush bones, killing the prey quickly.

Harpy eagle

An aye-aye has the largest hands of any primate – almost half the total length of their arms! To find food, aye-ayes tap on trees with their pointed claws and listen for a hollow sound, which would suggest an insect could be hiding inside. Then they use their exceptionally long, bony middle fingers to dig their meal out of the bark. The aye-aye's claws are so long they have to be curled up for climbing.

Frogs and toads lay eggs with a soft jelly envelope and no shell. A cane toad lays up to 35,000 eggs at a time!

Cane toad eggs

Peregrine falcon

A Giant Pacific octopus only lays eggs once in her life. She covers them with her body until they hatch, never moving, even to look for food. This can take more than four years!

Giant Pacific octopus

Southern Ocean giant sea spider

Crocodile eggs

Female python

Ocean sunfish eggs

Eggs-stravaganza!

Birds, fish, reptiles, amphibians and insects all lay eggs. There are two mammals that do too. All eggs do the same job, providing food and protection for a baby animal as it grows. But they come in millions of different sizes, shapes and colours. Eggs are just as varied as the animals that lay them!

Yellowheaded jawfish

American robin eggs

Leatherback turtle

Leatherback turtle eggs

Leatherback turtles lay leathery-shelled eggs that are almost perfectly round. Although the turtles live at sea, they return to land to lay their eggs, hiding them in sandy burrows to keep them warm.

Platypuses and echidnas are the only mammals in the world that lay eggs. Platypuses dig a burrow to keep their eggs warm, while echidnas keep their eggs in pouches on their belly.

Echidna

Platypus and eggs

Stink-bug eggs

The hard outside of an insect egg is called a chorion. It's often waxy, which stops the egg drying out.

African driver ant

Honeybee

Earth-boring beetle

Emperor penguin

The female emperor penguin lays the egg, but it is the male who keeps it warm and waits for it to hatch.

Can you spot an animal carrying her eggs on her legs, and an animal balancing an egg on his feet?

Eggs

A bird's eggshell is made of the same material as coral and seashells, and it is light but strong. Eggshells protect a growing baby bird from germs, but they are full of tiny holes, which let oxygen in. Usually, bigger birds lay bigger eggs and smaller birds lay smaller eggs. But plenty of birds break these rules!

Kiwis lay the biggest eggs for their size – each one is about a fifth of the weight of a fully grown kiwi! It takes around a month for the egg to grow. By the time it's ready, a female kiwi has no room left inside for food! Birds that lay eggs in holes, such as the kiwi, often have pale eggs that are easy for their parents to spot, so they don't get accidentally crushed.

North Island brown kiwi egg

Tufted ground squirrel

These ground squirrels have the world's bushiest tails. Each tail takes up almost a third more space than the squirrel's body. If you glimpsed it from a distance, you'd think the tail was the body and the body was the tail! This confuses predators such as clouded leopards, who prowl the forests where the squirrels live. After pouncing on what they think is a juicy squirrel, they end up with a mouthful of fluff!

Find out more!

To help us keep track, animals are organised into categories based on their features. Over the next few pages, discover the many fascinating features of the "mystery" animals scattered through this book.

Mammals

All mammals are warm-blooded, feed their young milk and have fur or hair. Did you know that YOU are a mammal? Mammals live on land and in water, from towering trees to deep oceans and dark caves. They range from tiny bumblebee bats to blue whales – the largest animals that have ever lived! Let's meet a few more mammals ...

Mammals use their tails for many things. **Red wolves** use their tails to signal to each other – a tail between the legs means that the animal is in no mood to fight!

A **woolly spider monkey** can use its long tail like a hand to grab onto things, and the female **common mouse opossum** can carry leaves with its tail.

Greater bilbys do not have good eyesight, but they make up for it with sharp hearing and a great sense of smell.

Most mammals can swivel their ears to work out where a sound is coming from. **Caracals** have 20 different muscles to help with this! A **sea otter** can "close" its ears when underwater.

The **antelope jackrabbit** and **fennec fox** lose heat through their enormous ears, which helps them keep cool. Most magnificent are the ears of a **long-eared jerboa**, two-thirds the length of its body!

The **aardvark** can close its nostrils to keep out dust and insects. The little **Pyrenean desman** has a different trick – its snout is a snorkel, letting it spend most of its time underwater.

By closing one nostril and blowing through the other, male **hooded seals** can inflate the skin at the end of their noses like a big red balloon. This helps them to attract a mate. **Mandrills** also have very clever noses – they can tell which of their group has a parasite infection by smelling its poo!

Large, flat teeth at the backs of their mouths help **zebras** to grind down the grasses they eat.

Despite its name, the **crabeater seal** does not actually eat crabs! Its strange-looking teeth are used to sieve tiny snacks from seawater.

The **common warthog** uses its sharp tusks to dig, fight and defend itself.

A **sun bear's** 25-cm-long tongue is perfect for reaching into beehives for honey. **Okapis** also have long tongues, and use them to wash around their own eyes!

A mammal's skin has lots of tricks to help control body temperature. The cracks and wrinkles on a **rhino's** skin trap water and dirt, helping these huge mammals to keep cool.

Fennec fox

Crabeater seal

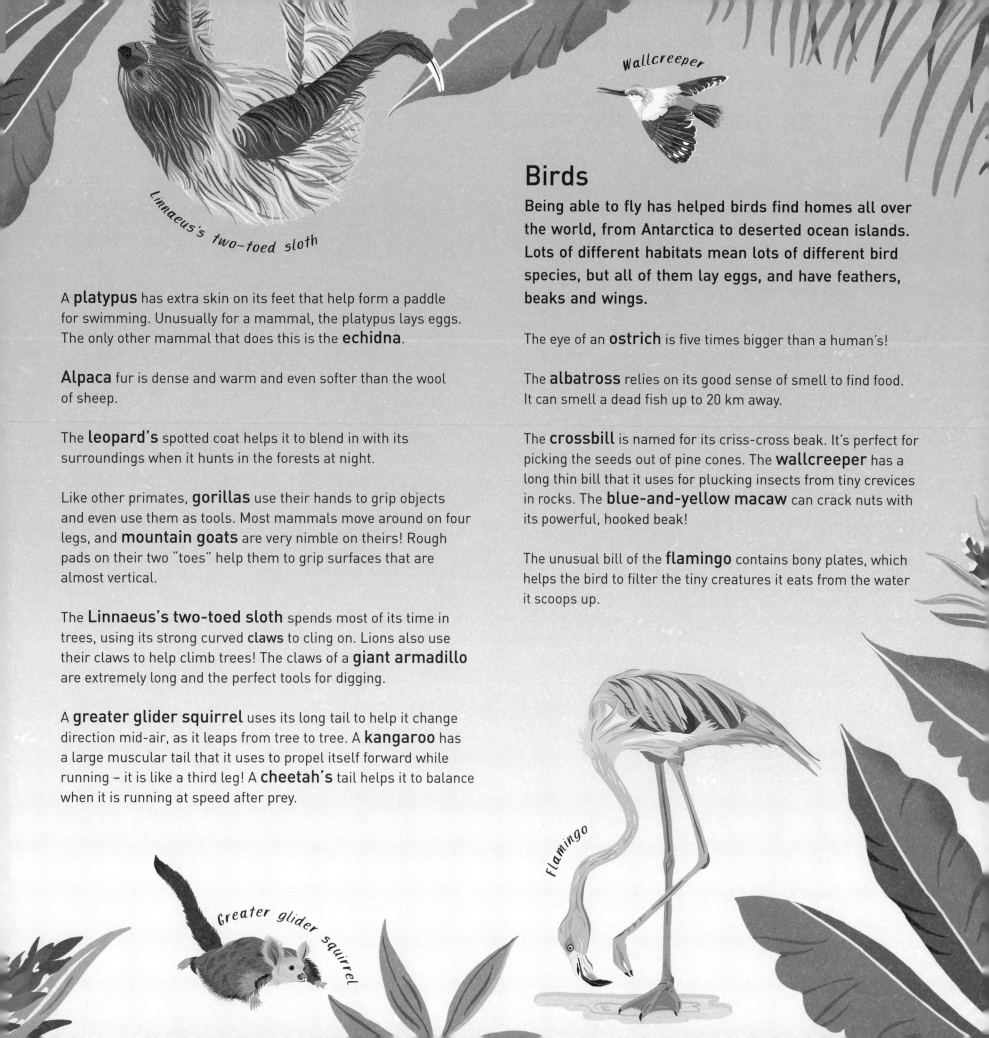

Linnaeus's two-toed sloth

Wallcreeper

Birds

Being able to fly has helped birds find homes all over the world, from Antarctica to deserted ocean islands. Lots of different habitats mean lots of different bird species, but all of them lay eggs, and have feathers, beaks and wings.

A **platypus** has extra skin on its feet that help form a paddle for swimming. Unusually for a mammal, the platypus lays eggs. The only other mammal that does this is the **echidna**.

The eye of an **ostrich** is five times bigger than a human's!

Alpaca fur is dense and warm and even softer than the wool of sheep.

The **albatross** relies on its good sense of smell to find food. It can smell a dead fish up to 20 km away.

The **leopard's** spotted coat helps it to blend in with its surroundings when it hunts in the forests at night.

The **crossbill** is named for its criss-cross beak. It's perfect for picking the seeds out of pine cones. The **wallcreeper** has a long thin bill that it uses for plucking insects from tiny crevices in rocks. The **blue-and-yellow macaw** can crack nuts with its powerful, hooked beak!

Like other primates, **gorillas** use their hands to grip objects and even use them as tools. Most mammals move around on four legs, and **mountain goats** are very nimble on theirs! Rough pads on their two "toes" help them to grip surfaces that are almost vertical.

The unusual bill of the **flamingo** contains bony plates, which helps the bird to filter the tiny creatures it eats from the water it scoops up.

The **Linnaeus's two-toed sloth** spends most of its time in trees, using its strong curved **claws** to cling on. Lions also use their claws to help climb trees! The claws of a **giant armadillo** are extremely long and the perfect tools for digging.

A **greater glider squirrel** uses its long tail to help it change direction mid-air, as it leaps from tree to tree. A **kangaroo** has a large muscular tail that it uses to propel itself forward while running – it is like a third leg! A **cheetah's** tail helps it to balance when it is running at speed after prey.

Greater glider squirrel

Flamingo

The bright, yellow and red markings on the **saddle-billed stork's** bill look just like a horse's saddle!

The **tawny frogmouth** has a wide mouth (just like a frog!) and a slightly hooked bill, which it uses to catch prey.

The **powerful** beak of a bald eagle is hooked to help it tear its food apart.

The **snowy egret** flickers its tongue on the surface of the water to attract small fish to the surface. The tongue of a **red-bellied woodpecker** is so long that it has to be stored wrapped around its skull, extending like a tape-measure to three times the length of its beak!

The **winged nightjar's** special feathers are used just for showing off to mates.

With its bright-purple head, and green, yellow, red and orange feathers, camouflage is not an option for the **rainbow lorikeet**. Instead, it hangs out in huge groups for protection.

The **emu** has wings but cannot fly. It has soft feathers on its body and stiff tail feathers.

The magnificent tail feathers of **Reeve's pheasant** can be more than 2 m long. Their only function is showing off! **Male peafowl** go one step further, spreading their tail feathers like a fan and shaking them to wow females.

Long toes and claws allow **long-legged jacana** to spread their weight as they walk on lily pads and other plants that grow on the surface of water.

Saddle-billed stork

Swifts spend most of their time in the air. They can even sleep whilst flying, resting half their brain at a time!

A **sparrow** may only have small wings, but it can fly fast in short bursts.

The wings of a **blue jay** have an "elliptical" shape, which help it fly about quickly from place to place in forest habitats

When a **peregrine falcon** dives from the air to catch its prey, it can reach speeds of up to 320 km per hour, making it the fastest living creature!

One of the world's highest-flying birds is the **Ruppell's griffin vulture**. It can fly high enough to peer in the windows of a jumbo jet.

A **gentoo penguin's** wings don't have flight feathers, but they are perfect for gliding underwater.

An **American robin's** eggs are an amazing bright blue. The colour comes from a special pigment in the female robin's blood.

Winged nightjar

Blue jay

Blue-tongued skink

Reptiles

These four-legged creatures have skin covered in scales and bony plates, and most of them lay eggs. Reptiles can't heat their own bodies, but rely on the sun's energy to stay warm enough to move around and digest their food. This is why most reptiles are found in warm parts of the world.

Chameleons have amazing eyes that can move in different directions at the same time, giving them an impressive range of vision! The **tuatara** has a third eye on top of its head! While it might help young tuatara to avoid predators, it's covered with skin by the time the animal is fully grown.

Pythons breathe through their noses but smell through their mouths! Scent particles in the air are detected on their tongue, just as we can detect particles inside our noses.

The knob on the end of an adult **gharial's** long thin snout is called a "ghara". When the male is courting a female, they blow bubbles out of it!

Small chameleons, such as the **rosette-nosed pygmy chameleon**, have the fastest-moving tongues in the animal kingdom! They use their extremely long sticky tongues to snatch insects.

Komodo dragons have forked tongues, just like snakes. They can also smell with their tongues! The **blue-tongued skink** sticks out its bright-blue tongue to scare predators away.

The colourful male **panther chameleon** can change its skin to a rainbow of colours. It does this to communicate feelings such as anger, or to attract a female mate.

A **frilled lizard** has a large flap of skin on its neck that it can open like an umbrella, making it look scarier to predators. The **Draco lizard** is also known as a flying dragon! It can glide from tree to tree by unfolding long ribs to stretch special folds of skin into "wings".

Reptiles such as the **African fire skink** have skin covered in scales. They protect the creatures from bumps and bites, and stop them drying out in hot weather.

Rosette-nosed pygmy chameleon

African fire skink

Leaf-tailed gecko

peacock treefrog

Amphibians

Most amphibians live in or near water because their skin dries out easily. There are advantages to being thin-skinned though – they can absorb water and breathe through their skin.

The large eyes of the **peacock tree frog** helps it to find prey at night.

The most poisonous skin belongs to the **golden poison arrow** frog. Its bright colour acts as a warning.

Most reptiles live in warm, damp places, such as tropical forests. By spreading its webbed toes, this **Wallace's flying frog** can glide from tree to tree!

The end of the **leaf-tailed gecko's** tail looks exactly like a dead leaf. This helps the tiny lizard to blend in with its surroundings and stay hidden from predators.

The **Madagascan collared iguana** uses its spiny tail to protect itself. If it is threatened, it will hide in a crevice in a tree and use its tail as a barrier.

The **Pallas glass snake** is really a lizard without legs! Like many lizards, it sometimes leaves its tail behind to trick predators. A new tail then grows in its place.

The **tokay gecko** has incredibly sticky toes that allow it to grip onto any surface – it can even climb up walls!

The **crocodile** has the strongest bite in the animal kingdom – so it's lucky it can grow new teeth when one gets wrenched out. Like most other reptiles, crocodiles lay eggs. If a baby crocodile struggles to hatch, the mother will gently crack the shell in its jaw.

Don't let the name fool you – the **African clawed frog** doesn't actually have claws! It has three toes on the back of each foot, and the tips of these toes are hardened and look like claws.

Salamanders have a strange superpower – they can drop their tails to distract a predator, and then grow a new one!

Nile crocodile

Salamander

Elephantnose fish

Long-spined porcupine fish

Fish

Fish have been on Earth far longer than mammals, birds, reptiles or amphibians! All fish live in water. They have fins to help them balance and steer, and gills that allow them to breathe underwater.

The **hammerhead shark** has an eye on each side of its strange, T-shaped head. This helps it to see all around.

Like all fish, the **goblin shark** smells with tiny pits, called "nares". Some fish have extra senses, too. The **elephantnose fish** can detect tiny electrical signals from the muscles of other creatures.

The fang-like teeth of the **viperfish** are so large that they overlap and stick out of its mouth, even when closed. The **wolf eel** has small spiky teeth, and a strong jaw to crush its prey.

The scales that cover a fish provide protection. The scales of the giant **Arapaima fish** are armour against piranha teeth!

Peacock flounders can change the colour of their scales to keep themselves safe. When they swim close to the surface, they become almost see-through, so they are harder for predators below to spot!

The **electric eel** generates its own electricity to stun its prey and to defend itself against any other animal that attempts to eat it.

When threatened, the **long-spined porcupine fish** will fill its body with water or air, so it looks like a ball. This causes its spines to stand on end, giving it a fearsome appearance!

Scales can act as camouflage. The markings on the scales of the **spotted wobbegong** help it to remain hidden in reefs and on rocky ocean floors.

The male **yellow-headed jawfish** carries the eggs in its mouth to keep them safe until they are ready to hatch.

Female **ocean sunfish** can release as many as 300 million eggs at one time!

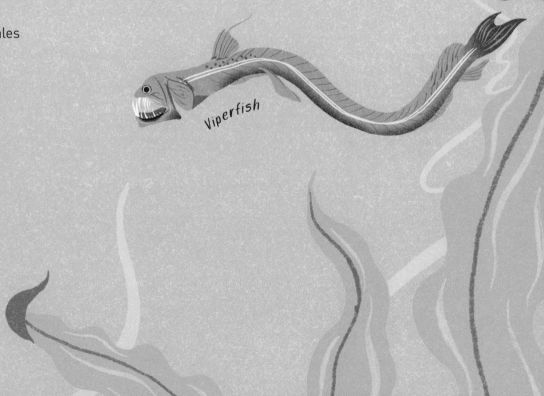
Viperfish

Peacock flounder

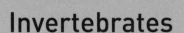
Honeybee

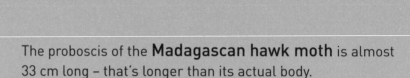
Madagascan hawk moth

Invertebrates

This huge group includes all animals without a backbone, including insects. Many have a hard, outer "exoskeleton" to protect their squidgy insides. More than three-quarters of all animals belong to a group called the arthropods. This includes insects, arachnids, centipedes, crustaceans, and other animals with bodies divided into segments and legs with joints.

The eyes of a **peacock mantis shrimp** are mounted on stalks. Each one is made up of thousands of tiny eyes, making them incredibly sensitive. They can see many more colours than humans can. A **cuttlefish's** eyes are more like a human's, but with unique, W-shaped pupils. However, cuttlefish cannot see any colours at all.

Most spiders have four pairs of eyes! In the **ogre-faced spider**, one pair is giant, helping it to hunt.

Insect sense organs are often found in very different places to those of vertebrates. **Grasshoppers** have "ears" on the sides of their bodies!

Greater wax moths can hear the very high-pitched clicks made by bats – so they can escape before the bats hear them!

The male **silk moth** does not have a nose, but can "smell" a female silk moth from up to 10 km away using very sensitive antennae on their heads.

Sea urchins have five incredibly sharp teeth – they can even bite through rock.

A **snail** is a mollusc, the second-biggest group of invertebrates after insects. Snails have over 14,000 microscopic teeth – on their tongues!

The **goliath bird-eating spider** is the largest spider in the world – and it has venomous fangs measuring 2.5 cm.

The proboscis of the **Madagascan hawk moth** is almost 33 cm long – that's longer than its actual body.

A beetle's scales are made of a material called chitin. The random arrangement of these scales can give the **iridescent scarab beetle** a very shiny appearance. The scales of **sugarcane white beetles** reflect all colours of light equally, making them look pure white – one of the brightest whites found in the natural world.

A **bumblebee** has four sets of wings. They are able to flap them an incredible 200 times a second! The **hummingbird hawkmoth** flaps its wings at such great speed that they make a humming sound.

The eggs of a **stink bug** are shaped like little barrels. Eggs are carefully laid side-by-side on the underside of leaves.

Honeybee colonies build complicated "honeycombs" to keep their eggs safe as they develop. Each hexagonal "cell" is home to a developing egg or larva, or is used to store honey and pollen to feed them.

African driver ant queens are some of the biggest egg layers in the world. One queen can lay millions of eggs every 25 days. No wonder she needs a whole colony of worker ants to look after them all!

You may not think of creepy-crawlies as caring parents, but they often protect their eggs fiercely. The **giant sea spider** carries her eggs around on her legs!

Many insects have body parts that stick out like a tail. The **common mayfly** has two or three! These long threads help to keep this delicate insect from wobbling too much as it flies.

Snail

Common mayfly

Glossary

Blue morpho butterfly

Swift

ADAPTED Changed over time to better suit the conditions

BLUBBER The fat of mammals that live in oceans, such as whales and seals

BREED To mate and have babies

CAMOUFLAGE Ability to hide by blending in with surroundings

CATAPULT Hurl or launch something

COMMUNICATE Share information, such as ideas or feelings

DISGUISE Look like someone or something else to stay hidden

EARDRUM Part of an animal's ear, which vibrates when sound waves reach it

EXOSKELETON Hard covering on the outside of the body of many animals, which protects and supports the animal

FANG A large, sharp tooth

FEMALE An animal that can lay eggs or produce babies from its body

HABITAT The natural home of a living thing

HATCH To break out of an egg

HOVER To stay in one place in the air

LENSES The part of an animal's eye that focuses light

MALE An animal that produces sperm, which can fertilise the eggs of females

MANDIBLES A word for the mouthparts of certain animals, especially mouthparts that can crush things

MATE When two animals come together in a way that allows sperm to fertilise eggs, which may then grow into baby animals

NAVIGATE To find the way

NECTAR A sweet, sugary liquid made by flowers to encourage insects to visit

PAPILLAE Small, spiny parts

POLLEN A fine powder produced by male parts of plants, which contains half of the instructions needed for a new plant to grow

PREDATOR An animal that hunts other animals for food

PRESSURE A pushing force

PREY An animal that is hunted or captured for food

PROBOSCIS The long tube-like mouthparts of a butterfly or moth

PUPIL The part of an animal's eye that lets in light into the eye

ROOST Where or when a bird or bat rests, especially at night

SALIVA The spit of an animal

SENSES The ways in which an animal finds out about its surroundings

SURROUNDINGS The objects and things happening around an animal

TOXIC Poisonous

VENOMOUS Creatures that can produce their own poison to cause injury or death to other animals

VIBRATIONS Shaking with tiny, repeated movements

WINGSPAN The distance between the tips of a pair of outstretched wings

Iridescent scarab beetle

For everyone at Egremont Primary School – I.T.

For Peta, my favourite drawing companion – D.C.

First published in Great Britain in 2022 by Wren & Rook

HB ISBN: 978 1 5263 6325 1
PB ISBN: 978 1 5263 6324 4
E-book ISBN: 978 1 5263 6326 8
10 9 8 7 6 5 4 3 2 1

MIX
Paper from
responsible sources
FSC
www.fsc.org   FSC® C104740

Wren & Rook
An imprint of
Hachette Children's Group
Part of Hodder & Stoughton
Carmelite House | 50 Victoria Embankment | London EC4Y 0DZ
An Hachette UK Company
www.hachette.co.uk
www.hachettechildrens.co.uk

Senior Commissioning Editor: Liza Wilde
Art Director: Laura Hambleton
Senior Editor: Sadie Smith
Senior Designer: Sophie Gordon

Printed in China

Marvel ® is a registered trade mark of Marvel Characters, Inc.